MY F
FRENCH
WORD
BOOK

Ruth Thomson
Photography by Mike Galletly

Conran Octopus

Jouez avec nous
Come and play with us

le lapin
rabbit

le clown
clown

la poupée
doll

le puzzle
puzzle

l'appareil photo
camera

l'ours
bear

**la poupée
de chiffon**
rag doll

la boîte aux lettres
post box

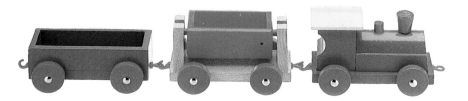

la locomotive et les wagons
engine and trucks

4

Dans la cabane
In the den

le marteau
hammer

le tournevis
screwdriver

la radio
radio

la poêle à frire
frying pan

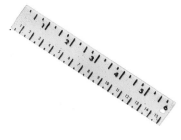

la règle
ruler

les pinces
pliers

la clé plate
spanner

**les boulons et
les écrous**
nuts and bolts

la casserole
saucepan

le téléphone
telephone

À la plage
At the beach

le râteau
rake

le tamis
sieve

le ballon
ball

le drapeau
flag

la pelle
spade

**les lunettes
de soleil**
sunglasses

le voilier
yacht

le moule
mould

le seau
bucket

la benne
dump truck

Imaginez . . .
Let's pretend

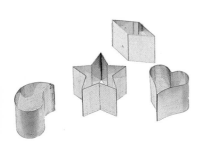

les emportes-pièces
pastry cutters

le perroquet
parrot

le plumier
pencil box

le rouleau à pâtisserie
rolling pin

le sifflet
whistle

le cahier
exercise book

la casquette
cap

les craies
chalk

les lunettes de moto
goggles

le coffre
treasure chest

À l'hôpital
At the hospital

le raisin
grapes

le médicament
medicine

la feuille de température
temperature chart

le sparadrap
plaster

la gaze
bandage

Bon rétablissement!
Get well soon!

les ciseaux
scissors

le thermomètre
thermometer

le coton
cotton wool

la bouillotte
hot-water bottle

Au jardin
In the garden

les bottes
boots

**la fourche
à main**
fork

la brouette
wheelbarrow

la fleur
flower

le pot de fleurs
flowerpot

la chaise longue
deckchair

la pelle
trowel

les graines
seeds

la ficelle
string

l'arrosoir
watering can

Bon anniversaire!
Happy birthday!

le ballon
balloon

le mirliton
party blower

le gâteau d'anniversaire
birthday cake

l'assiette
plate

le cake
fairy cake

le chapeau
hat

le serpentin
streamer

la tasse
cup

le sandwich
sandwich

le cadeau
present

L'heure du bain
Bath time

l'essuie-mains
flannel

le talc
powder

le canard
duck

le savon
soap

le dauphin
dolphin

la serviette de bain
towel

le shampooing
shampoo

l'éponge
sponge

la brosse à cheveux
hairbrush

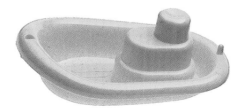

le bateau
boat

Avant de se coucher
Time for bed

le miroir
mirror

**la chemise
de nuit**
nightdress

**la robe
de chambre**
dressing gown

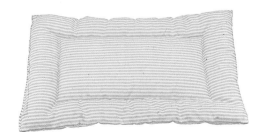

l'édredon
quilt

l'oreiller
pillow

le tableau
picture

le biberon
bottle

**le fauteuil
à bascule**
rocking chair

les pantoufles
slippers

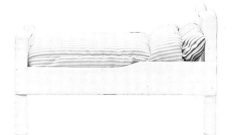

le lit
bed

How to say the French words

Some sounds in the French language are quite different from any in English. This is a very simple pronunciation guide. If you read the words as if they were English, you will be close to French pronunciation! Here are a few guidelines:

a(n) and o(n)—the n is not spoken, but the vowel before it is pronounced through the nose and the mouth; there is no sound like this in English;

e(r)—the e sounds like the e in over or the (not thee); the r is not spoken;

ew—again, there is no similar English sound; to pronounce it, round your lips and try to say ee;

j—is said like s in measure;

r—is said by rolling the r in the back of the mouth.

● appareil photo	a-pa-ray fo-toe
arrosoir	a-ro-zwar
assiette	a-see-et
● ballon	ba-lo(n)
bateau	ba-toe
benne	ben
biberon	bee-bro(n)
boîte aux lettres	bwat o let-tr
bon rétablissement	bo(n) ray-ta-blees-ma(n)
bottes	bot
bouillotte	boo-ee-yot
boulons	boo-lo(n)
brosse à cheveux	bross a she(r)—ve(r)
brouette	broo-et
● cabane	ca-ban
cadeau	ca-doe
cahier	ca-yay
cake	cayk
canard	ca-nar
casquette	cass-ket
casserole	cass-rol
chaise longue	shayz lo(n)g
chapeau	sha-po
chemise de nuit	she(r)-meez de(r) nwee
ciseaux	see-zo
clé plate	clay plat
clown	cloon
coffre	cof-fr
coton	co-to(n)
craies	cray
● dauphin	doe-fa(n)
drapeau	dra-po
● écrous	ay-croo
édredon	ay-dre(r)-do(n)
emportes-pièces	a(n)-port-pee-ess
éponge	ay-po(n)j
essuie-mains	ess-wee-ma(n)
● fauteuil à bascule	fo-te(r)-ye(r) a bas-cewl
feuille de température	fe(r)y de(r) ta(n)-pay-ra-tewr
ficelle	fee-sell
fleur	fler
fourche à main	foorsh a ma(n)
● gâteau d'anniversaire	ga-toe da-nee-vair-sair
gaze	gaz
graines	grain
● hôpital	op-ee-tal
● jardin	jar-da(n)
● lapin	la-pa(n)
lit	lee
locomotive	lock-om-ot-eev
lunettes de moto	lew-net de(r) mo-toe
lunettes de soleil	lew-net de(r) sol-ay
● marteau	mar-toe
médicament	may-dee-ca-ma(n)
mirliton	meer-lee-to(n)
miroir	meer-war
moule	mool
● oreiller	or-ay-ay
ours	oors
● pantoufles	pa(n)-too-fl
pelle	pell
perroquet	pay-rock-ay
pinces	pa(n)s
plage	plaj
plumier	plew-mee-ay
poêle à frire	pwal a freer
pot de fleurs	po de(r) fler
poupée	poo-pay
poupée de chiffon	poo-pay de(r) shee-fo(n)
puzzle	pew-zl
● radio	ra-dee-o
raisin	ray-sa(n)
râteau	ra-toe
règle	ray-gl
robe de chambre	rob de(r) sha(n)-br
rouleau à pâtisserie	roo-lo a pa-tees-ree
● sandwich	sa(n)d-weetsh
savon	sa-vo(n)
seau	so
serpentin	sair-pa(n)-ta(n)
serviette de bain	sair-vee-et de(r) ba(n)
shampooing	sha(n)-pwa(n)
sifflet	see-flay
sparadrap	spa-ra-dra
● tableau	tab-lo
talc	talc
tamis	ta-mee
tasse	tass
téléphone	tay-lay-fon
thermomètre	tair-mom-ay-tr
tournevis	toor-ne(r)-veece
● voilier	vwal-yay
● wagons	va-go(n)